ideals® EASTER

On Easter the bells in the steeples greet the spring morning, and the white bells of the lilies lift their soundless music of praise and beauty. But the sweetest bells of all are those that ring in the heart.

—ESTHER YORK BURKHOLDER

IDEALS PUBLICATIONS

NASHVILLE, TENNESSEE

Spring Pools
Robert Frost

These pools that, though in forests, still reflect
The total sky almost without defect,
And like the flowers beside them, chill and shiver,
Will like the flowers beside them soon be gone,
And yet not out by any brook or river,
But up by roots to bring dark foliage on.

The trees that have it in their pent-up buds
To darken nature and be summer woods—
Let them think twice before they use their powers
To blot out and drink up and sweep away
These flowery waters and these watery flowers
From snow that melted only yesterday.

Spring
Louise Hajek

In emerald shoes Spring pirouettes
Upon a crystal stage,
Then lifts enchanting hands to free
A singing scarlet page.

From barren stalks she draws bright flags
As sun spotlights her art,
And with a violet-scented kiss
She melts King Winter's heart.

Spring Freshet
Grace Noll Crowell

I like the look of snow when it is melting
And sending its clear rivulets toward the sea;
I like the sweep of dry grasses bending
Beneath those bright feet, suddenly set free.

I have seen small green leaves under water
That snow had hidden through the winter hours,
Fresher and greener and sweeter than the leafing
That springs to life after the April showers:

A little clover leaf washed clean by waiting,
Eager for life again at the hint of spring!
I reach my fingers into the icy water
To touch that tender, tremulous, wistful thing,

Knowing a kinship with it, deep and abiding,
I, too, have waited until the winter passed,
And I lift my head after a strange chastisement
To the bright air again, the sun at last!

The Flowers of Easter

Nancy Byrd Turner

They have come back to field
   and hill,
To garden and to wood,
The crocus and the daffodil,
The violet in her hood,
The mignonette, the pansy blue,
The lily straight and tall—
So like the flowers, dewy, still,
In that old garden on a hill,
The first Easter of all!

I think the light that morning fell
In the same lovely way
On petal, leaf, and lifting bell,
As the light falls today;
That violets looked gently up,
Hearing the dawn-wind's call,
And dew was in a crocus cup
And fragrance in a lily cup,
In that old garden long ago,
The first Easter of all.

PRECIOUS AS ARE ALL THE SEASONS OF THE year, none so rejoices
the heart as spring. There is about spring a gladness that thrills the
soul and lifts it up into regions of spiritual sunshine. —*Helen Keller*

A Lady Red—Amid the Hill

Emily Dickinson

A Lady red—amid the Hill
Her annual secret keeps!
A Lady white, within the Field
In placid Lily sleeps!

The tidy Breezes, with their Brooms
Sweep vale—and hill—and tree!
Prithee, My pretty Housewives,
Who may expected be?

The Neighbors do not yet suspect!
The Woods exchange a smile!
Orchard and Buttercup and Bird—
In such a little while!

And yet, how still the Landscape stands!
How nonchalant the Hedge!
As if the "Resurrection"
Were nothing very strange!

What Is Spring?

Sam Churchill

Spring is a precise and delicate thing.

It is the touch of pink in an apricot bloom, the golden smile of a daffodil, water in an irrigation canal, the sound of a tractor in a field.

It is the way you feel when you get up in the morning, the glint of sunlight on a windowsill, the underground noise robins hear as worms work their way below the surface of a lawn.

Spring is yellowish twine strung from overhead wires to ground stakes around a vegetable garden; it's lambs dozing in the sun.

Spring is a farmer sifting soil between his fingers, weeds burning along a road, a housecat watching a bird.

Spring is seed going into the ground; it is the laughter of children.

It is big, fluffy clouds coasting across the sky, raindrops making rings in a puddle.

Spring isn't something you check out on a calendar or are alerted to by the *Farmer's Almanac*. It's suddenly being able to bend over with ease and tie your shoes in the morning. It's going inside the house and forgetting to shut the door. It's taking a handful of bills from the mailbox without making a single remark to your wife.

Spring is when you dream of tomorrow and enjoy today. It's when you forget to turn on the television.

It's a gentle stirring deep inside that insists you walk instead of waiting for a bus.

It's that fleeting moment of time each year when you suddenly become you.

It's when you say, "Good morning," and mean it.

It's a moment of goodwill and pleasant thoughts.

It's when God speaks and you can hear Him.

Photograph © Maresol/Shutterstock Images

#5 Chickadee Ln.

In Spring

Eileen Spinelli

In spring
I lean into
the tender slant of light,
into a feathered song,
the hum of bee,
into the yellow tumble of a bush,
into the greening of the willow tree.

In spring
I lean away from littered snow,
from battered ice,
and wisps of worried wings.

In spring
I lean into
the scent of sun
and wrap my heart around
more hopeful things.

CHICKADEE LANE *by Janene Grende.*
Image © Janene Grende/Wild Wings
(www.wildwings.com)

After the Rain

Anna Johnson

Meadow larks
From the boughs
Of new-green birches
Dripping silver,
Fresh from the recent rain,
Whistle in the pearl-gray light
Of evening.
The joy of the chorus
Swells in a blaze
Flaming splendor,
While the fragrance
Of song
Is borne
Into space.

Spring Washing

Norma Wrathall

How clean the sky has washed her face
In rain that lasted through the night—
And on the mountain peaks has pinned
Her winter's washing, snowy white!
But clothes of dainty pastel shade
She draped on loops the rainbow made.

*Marsh marigolds after a rain. Photograph ©
R Sherwood Veith/iStockPhoto*

Kite Rite

Elizabeth Wells

Kite-flying is a venerable spring tradition, but in our family it also has religious significance. Every Easter, after the last egg is found and church clothes are hung, our family gathers kites, tails, and string and heads to the nearest open field. In the Midwest, this can mean skipping in light jackets or tromping through leftover snow in bundled layers to keep chilly blasts from rattling our bones. Either way, it marks an official, if sometimes defiant, welcome to spring's promises of new life.

There is an almost palpable hope as each family member prepares to launch a kite. In fact, I have found that kite-flying parallels Good Friday's anticipation of Jesus' victory over death. I'm not alone. For more than a century, the people of Bermuda have made kite flying their Good Friday tradition. Island lore has it that a Sunday school teacher or missionary once illustrated Christ's Ascension by flying a kite, then cutting its string so it disappeared

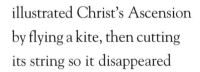

into the sky. Christians in other European countries observe similar customs on Easter Monday.

While kite-flying is a good illustration of the Ascension, I see similarities between the act of flying a kite and our human and spiritual journey toward resurrection. It also resembles our hope and desire to be caught by God's love and lifted to heights unimaginable.

Anyone who's flown a kite knows they don't typically go up in a straight line. They meander left and right—even in loops. The spiritual journey can feel like this. There are times when I become complacent. I think I have mastered the angles, and it becomes blasé. The kite, or my faith-walk, continues but lacks heart. Things can fall because I am not paying attention.

Catching the wind is tricky business, an exercise in faith. The force of a gentle breeze or strong blast cannot be seen. The outstretched flag or swaying trees prove that the wind exists because they have been touched. It reminds me that we are called to give proof of God's existence.

Sometimes the wind, without warning, seems to disappear completely, and the kite falls. Quick tugs on the string may reconnect it to the wind. Other times a full-scale sprint in the opposite direction is necessary. Sometimes nothing can be done to alter the course. It can be frustrating.

The wind, like God's presence, can seem to be everywhere except where I am. Others seem to be sailing along effortlessly. These are times I must return to the beginning. I need to check my position, angle, speed, then wait again at the taut-string stage. When the kite returns to the air, I'm filled with wonder and hope.

Kite-flying can also be a metaphor of the need for community. Releasing a kite can be done solo but is easier with another's help. Even as the string is stretched taut between the one who will gently toss the kite into the wind and the one holding the reel, excitement seems to travel down the line. It's play, but everyone sees the benefits of bearing one another's burdens.

When our children were younger, my husband and I purchased a kite that resembled a package of rainbow-colored crayons. The kite was quick to get airborne and became a springboard for talking about Jesus' Resurrection, Ascension, and the Holy Spirit's "rainbow" gifts. The lack of a rigid frame meant it didn't break when landing.

Illustration © Ideals Publications

Over the years we have added kites to our collection. Some were fancy and colorful, multi-layered contraptions that would have been incredible spectacles if we could only get them into the sky. Others were fragile and tore if the wind was too strong.

Last year our family decided to check out the newfangled and very fast stunt kites. The shop owner wowed our now young adult children with the kites' tricks and gave instructions for proper handling.

But on Easter we struggled with the powerful kites. They crashed with incredible force and frequency. Before long someone retrieved the old crayon kite from the trunk. Although it didn't do the tricks the stunt kites promised, it did go up, reminding us of the importance of simplicity.

Our desire is to rise above our human tendency to fall; we need God's help to soar on our journey to new life.

When It Is Easter

Helen Harrington

It is Easter now that hills
Are adorned with daffodils,
Now that ivory lilies grace
The garden pot and altar vase.

It is Easter now that spires
Shine with sunlight,
     now that choirs
Sing "Hallelujah!"
     and we come
In the faith of Christendom:

Believing love is twice as great
As suspicion, fear, and hate,
That the stony, angry door
Opens up to trust once more;

Believing too,
     that when we find
Joy supreme in being kind
And acknowledge
     peace sublime,
It is truly Eastertime!

SEE! THE WINTER IS PAST;
     the rains are over and gone.
Flowers appear on the earth;
     the season of singing has come,
     the cooing of doves
     is heard in our land.
     —*Song of Solomon 2:11–12 (NIV)*

On Easter Morn

Marion Doyle

As I arose on Easter morn
The dawn was barely gray;
The trees with branches upward borne
Seemed welcoming of day.

As I walked out on Easter morn
I saw the sun up-winging,
And on a jeweled clump of thorn,
A cardinal was singing.

As I walked out . . . as I walked out
Upon the Easter morning,
Beauty girded all about,
Lost were grief and grudge and doubt,
As joyfully the bells rang out
The triumph of that dawning.

Easter Morning

Kay Hoffman

I watched a lily from the barren sod
Lift up a pure white bloom to God;
A robin came at break of dawn
And sang his joyous morning song.

Sweet blossom scent, like incense rare,
Imbued the dew-drenched morning air;
The soft pink mist of dawn made way
For the sun's first golden ray.

On a hillside near so lately bare,
A dogwood tree bloomed wondrous fair;
God had the springtime world adorned
For this, His Resurrection morn.

Ephraim Moravian Church in Door County, Wisconsin.
Photograph © Ken Dequaine Photography

The Splendor of Lilies

Margaret E. Sangster

Oh, rare as the splendor of lilies
And sweet as the violet's breath
Comes the jubilant morning of Easter,
The triumph of life over death.
And fresh from the earth's
    quickening bosom
Full baskets of flowers we bring,
And scatter their satin soft petals
To carpet a path for our King.

In the countless green blades
    of the meadow,
The sheen of the daffodil's gold,
In the tremulous blue of the mountains,
The opaline mist on the wold,

In the tinkle of brooks through
    the pasture,
The river's strong sweep to the sea,
Are signs of the day that is hasting
In gladness to you and to me.

Oh, dawn in thy splendor of lilies,
Thy fluttering violet breath,
Oh, jubilant morning of Easter,
Thou triumph of life over death!
Then fresh from the earth's
    quickened bosom
Full baskets of flowers we bring,
And scatter their satin soft petals
To carpet a path for our King.

Walk in the Garden at Easter

Minnie Klemme

Come, walk in the garden at Easter
And see the lilies in bloom.
Recall how our crucified Savior
Stepped forth from the depths
    of the tomb.

In the chaliced heart of the lily
Rests a crown that is lovely to see,
Not unlike the crown which the Savior
Will wear through Eternity.

The lilies were there all about Him,
Supporting Him all through the night.

They, too, had conquered the darkness
As they rose with the coming of light.

In the beauty of springtime flowers,
Feel the tug that is light and is life.
The cross and the crown have
    new meaning
In the spring when the lilies are rife.

Come, walk in the garden at Easter,
Your life and your light to renew,
For the Gardener who cares for the lilies
As tenderly cares for you.

Easter Preparations

Helen Colwell Oakley

Chances are that we will have a beautiful Easter morning to model our very special fashions, as Easter comes late this year. The long winter has become a bit weary, and we are most eager to get on with spring.

We have been searching for signs of spring for ever-so-long, and finally we have found it. The frozen brook has changed into a babbling brook, the snow on the mountainside is slowly disappearing, and the tiny wildflowers will soon be ready to dress the mountain for its spring look.

And the spring look is upon *us*. The fashion shops are alive with fabulous creations. The florist's shop and the greenhouses are so breathtakingly beautiful with blooming plants. Fashion magazines are going all out to entice. To many, Easter is an Easter bonnet—casting aside the warm, sensible hat for a superb masterpiece, looking for all the world like a mini–English garden sitting atop milady's head.

Listen to the tolling of the bells ringing out in the stillness of the early morn. It's Easter morning! The services and cantatas are beautiful and much appreciated.

Do you observe the family customs and tradi-

tions handed down through the years at Eastertime? When I was growing up, Easter was a most fascinating time for our family. After church there was a large dinner with my mother's famous baked ham (glazed with brown sugar), mashed potatoes, buttered peas, cabbage salad, baking powder biscuits, brown bread, and an Easter cake with jellybeans on top. Mom and Dad gave each of us children a basket filled with colored Easter eggs, chocolate bunnies, jellybeans, and yellow marshmallow chickens. Best of all, each of us had a huge chocolate egg with his or her name drawn in frosting on top.

We had a large family of grandparents and aunts and uncles, so we received several small baskets filled with fancy decorated eggs and candies. There were six girls in my family. Can you imagine the Easter finery? We had organdy dresses, ruffled petticoats, and black patent leather sandals. Dad was so proud of us when we were all dressed up.

To me, spring has really sprung with the arrival of the Easter church services, festive baked ham dinners, little baskets filled with bunnies and colored eggs, and a fabulous whirl of fashionably dressed people in their Easter parades.

Photograph © Masterfile Corporation

Mother's Yellow Easter Dress
J. Evelyn Smith

While glancing through the album, an old one I confess,
I saw my mother's picture, taken in her yellow Easter dress.
How well I can remember when she wore it, many years ago—
A vision of loveliness, her features all aglow.

She had fashioned it with loving care and sewn for several weeks
To achieve that chic perfection, which every woman seeks.
She refused to let us see it, for it wasn't even worn
Until she made her entrance down the stairs that Easter morn.

We were standing there, just waiting, in our Easter Sunday best;
Even Father stood there quietly, but suspenseful as the rest.
His blue eyes never wavered, and a smile lit up his face
When Mother started downward at her usual graceful pace.

We stared in childish wonder as she stopped at Father's side,
For Mother walked in beauty—every heart filled up with pride.
The golden trim of ribbon and the lace so creamy white
Gave her yellow dress an elegance of Eastertime delight.

I'm glad I saw that certain picture of my mother once again,
Because it brought back memories of happy times; but then,
I never do regret the time it takes to sit and look
At old and treasured albums—they're a picture storybook.

Photograph © Daniel Dempster

Easter Sunday Cherub
Marian Paust

Caught by the glamour
Of her Easter gown,
She walks sedately
With her head bent down.

Her eyes follow closely
The quick come-and-go
Of each new gleaming
Patent leather toe.

Bonnets and Blossoms
Alice Leedy Mason

Along the rain-washed avenues
The hearts are light and gay,
For winter's spell is broken now,
And spring is here to stay.

Miracles are everywhere;
The air is warm and sweet.
Flower vendors sell their wares
On every busy street.

The beauty of the season starts
The poet writing sonnets,
And city streets are blooming, too,
With scores of Easter bonnets.

"The Worst Picker-Outer in the World"

Michelle Medlock Adams

At ages seven and five, Abby and Allyson were very particular about the way they looked—especially on Easter Sunday. They each had very distinctive opinions about what was cool and what was not. Pretty much anything I liked fell into the latter category. So I chose my battles wisely, and the rest of the time I let the girls make their own choices in hairstyles, clothing, and accessories. (Of course, I drew the line when Ally wanted to wear her ballerina costume to school, but normally they did a pretty good job of picking out their outfits.)

Even though the girls didn't always get it right, I discovered that one is never too old to learn a thing or two. I was, however, confident in a few fashion rules that I had learned from years of dressing myself—rules that were foreign to Abby and Allyson—such as: "Never wear white before Memorial Day," and "Black goes with everything." These sometimes triggered fashion fights in our home, such as the one that took place on a sunny Easter morning in March. As I helped Allyson buckle her dress shoes, I noticed that Abby was putting on shoes that I hadn't picked out for her.

"Ab, where are your black patent leather shoes?" I asked.

"In my closet."

"Why aren't they on your feet?" I inquired, staring at the white sparkly Little Mermaid sandals she had chosen.

"Because white goes better with my dress," Abby explained.

"But Abby, it's too early in the year to wear white. Plus, your Little Mermaid shoes are too casual for your beautiful Easter dress. And besides, honey, your feet will get cold," I coached. "You need to wear your black shiny shoes."

"But, Mom, black doesn't go with pink," Abby protested.

"That's not true," I said. "Black goes with everything. They'll look beautiful with your dress; now go put them on."

"Uggghhhhh," Abby groaned. "You are the worst picker-outer in the whole world!"

Well, I'd held many titles in my lifetime, but this was a new one for me. Halfway amused and halfway offended, I went to the car to wait for Jeff and the girls to join me.

Why won't she trust me? I thought. *Doesn't she know that I really do know best? Doesn't she respect me anymore? Why does she constantly challenge me?*

The questions flooded my mind. Just as I was about to answer the questions myself, lick my wounds, and pout a while, God interrupted my thoughts with His still, small voice deep down in my heart.

This is just the beginning. Your girls are going to make their own decisions about many things in life—things much more important than fashion—and you won't always be able to make them do what you want them to do.

That scared me because I knew it was true. With my girls aged seven and five, the time was coming when I would no longer have total control. It was coming more quickly than I liked.

You are going to have to give them to Me.

I was somewhat hurt by God's words to me. I thought I had already given my daughters to Him. I mean, I had even spoken those very words at their baby dedications in front of a whole assembly of people. The Holy Spirit began showing me that I hadn't really given them to God. I had allowed God to borrow them from time to time, but I had always taken them back.

To be honest, I was afraid to give my children fully to God, thinking He might not parent them as well as I could. Isn't that ridiculous thinking? It was much more ridiculous than Abby not trusting me to know which shoes looked best with her pink dress, though I hated to admit it.

During those few minutes alone in the car, I cried out before God. "I want to trust You, God, but what if You call them to foreign countries to be missionaries? What if You call them into dangerous professions? What if You allow them to make mistakes that I could help prevent?"

Then I heard God's tender voice asking the very questions about me that I'd asked about Abby moments before: *Why won't she trust Me? Doesn't she know that I really do know best? Doesn't she respect Me anymore? Why does she constantly challenge Me?*

That Easter morning, sitting in the car by myself, I truly gave my girls to God. It was one of the hardest things I have ever done, and it continues to be difficult. I find that I have to give Abby and Allyson to Him daily because if I don't, I'll take them right back again.

I realize that my girls won't always make decisions that I agree with or even approve of, but who's to say that I'm always going to be right? I don't think I could stand knowing that one of my poor decisions adversely affected my girls. You know, when I really think about it, it's a big relief to put that responsibility on God's shoulders—I don't have to worry, because He is in control of their lives. If they make a mistake, I might not be able to fix it, but God can and He promises that He will. So you see, giving our children to God is the best gift we could ever give them. Better than new Easter dresses and shiny shoes. Better than Easter baskets filled with candy. Better than anything.

My girls are teenagers now. Long gone are the days of frilly pink dresses and sparkly white Little Mermaid shoes. And, yes, at times, I'm still considered "the worst picker-outer in the world"—especially when shopping for Homecoming ensembles, prom gowns, and even Easter dresses. But one thing I chose correctly is when I gave my girls to God that Easter Sunday long ago. I don't care if your children are seven or seventy; it's not too late to turn them over to our Heavenly Father. So give your children to God this Easter and celebrate the season with renewed joy and peace.

Easter Jewels

Mildred Spires Jacobs

With polka dots of emerald green
And stripes of pink and jade,
A lovely work of artistry
From just an egg is made.

Another dipped in amethyst
And touched with golden hue
May sport a bit of deep cerise
And bands of turquoise blue.

An oval egg of ruby red
And scallops traced in white,
Accented by a cross of gold
Becomes a gorgeous sight.

A fragile topaz-colored egg
That sapphire trim bedecks,
Enhanced with deep, rich garnet drops
May shine with silver flecks.

Now brilliant in their many hues
Like jewels on display,
They wait in sparkling splendor for
A festive Easter Day.

The Puzzle of Easter

Pamela Kennedy

In many ways, Easter is a puzzling kind of holiday. On the one hand we have the solemn and beautiful biblical story of life triumphing over death in the Resurrection of Christ. On the other we have pastel Easter bunnies and Technicolor eggs. As a youngster, I remember trying to reconcile the empty tomb with an egg-laying rabbit and deciding that the only true thing about Easter was that you could never tell what was going to happen.

And that was certainly true in my family. For example, at Easter, my mother, a woman normally obsessed with safety and tidiness (at her insistence I wore an apron to breakfast every school day from the time I was five until I graduated high school) allowed me to not only boil eggs but also color them with permanent dye! We bought a kit at the grocery store; back then it was pretty simple: for twenty-nine cents you got six colored tablets and a piece of wire to be bent and used as an egg holder. Mom poured boiling water and a tablespoon of vinegar into each of six cups, and I dropped in the tablets and watched the water turn colors—red, blue, yellow, green, orange, and purple. Then, using the wire holder, I dunked a boiled egg into each cup. After a few minutes, I'd fish out the egg and set it to dry in the cardboard carton. I'm still not sure why I thought this was so exciting, but I can recall looking at the whole carton of brightly colored eggs, certain that I had accomplished something quite magical. After the eggs were dyed and tucked away in the fridge, the Easter Bunny, a creature I heard a lot about but never actually saw, showed up in the wee hours of Easter morning, removed the eggs from the refrigerator, and "layed" them all over the house. It never occurred to me to wonder how a rabbit could even open the huge Kelvinator in our kitchen, let alone conceal a dozen eggs.

Easter breakfast featured another incongruity. My mother, an early devotee of nutritionist Adelle Davis, abandoned wheat germ, brewer's yeast, and steel-cut oats for sugary hot-cross buns. I can still recall how the warm, spicy rolls, bursting with plump raisins and topped with a thick frosting cross, melted in my mouth. Breakfast finished, it was time to don my new Easter outfit, including hat, gloves, and shiny new patent-leather shoes. A few weeks before Easter, Mom and I went to Murray's Dry Goods Store and chose a pattern from the huge Simplicity catalog, then carefully examined the bolts of fabric. Whereas school clothes featured sturdy cottons and wools in colors least likely to show stains, my Easter dress was a completely impractical pastel in sheer organza or lacy eyelet, supported with layered petticoats. Daddy, who normally didn't accompany us to church, always went on Easter. There, accompanied by Mrs. Myrtle Beamans on the pipe organ, he belted out "Christ the Lord Is Risen Today" with a conviction he usually reserved for his favorite Frank Sinatra ballads. It was a completely otherworldly experience. As the morning sunlight streamed through the stained glass and the soloist sang "I Come to the Garden Alone," I inhaled the heady scent of lilies

PLAYED OUT—CATS *by Persis Clayton Weirs.*
Image © Persis Clayton Weirs/Wild Wings (www.wildwings.com)

and pretended I was there with Mary on that first Easter morning.

After church we hurried home to put the final touches on Easter dinner: baked ham, scalloped potatoes, creamed peas, and Easter bunny pear salads. The salads were my favorite because making them came perilously close to something I usually got scolded for: playing with my food.

On beds of shredded lettuce "grass," I nestled canned pear halves. A dollop of cottage cheese at the large ends of the pears created bunny tails, and sliced almonds stuck into the smaller ends served for ears. The eyes were currants and the noses, bits of maraschino cherry. An only child, I was accustomed to small, quiet dinners. But on Easter, noisy family members encircled the table. Conversation swirled like a comforting breeze as cousins, aunts, uncles, and Grandma shared stories of past and present. At the end of the meal,

we kids each received a foil-wrapped chocolate rabbit. Then we congregated in my bedroom where, devoid of adult supervision, we perched on the floor or the bed, bit the hollow ears off our bunnies, stuck them on our fingers as puppets, and made up ridiculous plays about "Rabbit World." At the end of the day everyone went home replete with food and replenished with faith.

And maybe that's the central truth in the midst of Easter's paradox: emptiness becomes full. Empty homes are filled with loving family members; empty baskets are filled with eggs; the empty tomb bursts with new life. And in the end the most important thing isn't to be able to explain it all, but just to understand that hope is discovered in the most unlikely places, and that Easter always surprises us with unexpected joy!

Faith Reborn

Reginald Holmes

Faith has rebirth when one perceives
The swelling buds and tiny leaves;
When daffodils and tulips creep
From beds that held them fast asleep.
The new grass prints its first designs
As south winds whisper in the pines.
The woodlot holds a feathered throng,
And nature's choir bursts forth in song.

How can one doubt when he beholds
The loveliness that spring unfolds?
For now through Easter's open door
Comes faith man never knew before.
For when God makes the seasons pass
And lifts again each blade of grass,
We surely know that mortal clay
Will have its resurrection day!

IT IS NOT THE VARIEGATED COLORS, THE CHEERFUL SOUNDS, and the warm breezes which enliven us so much in spring, as it is the quiet prophetic spirit of endless hope, a presentiment of many happy days, the anticipation of higher everlasting blossoms and fruits, and the secret sympathy with the world that is developing itself.

—Martin Opitz von Boberfeld

Easter Came to Me

Lucille Crumley

Easter enters every church,
She sits in every pew
And flaunts her ribboned bonnet
Flowered with every hue.

Easter enters every church,
She walks down every aisle,
But I met her in the early dawn
In my newborn's smile.

I saw her when she gently passed
Through a meadow of pure jade
And walked awhile with me beneath
The feathered plum tree's shade.

I watched her dance into the wind
Against the pink-skirted orchard trees.
We listened to a meadowlark
In a sun-bright April breeze.

Easter came to church today,
But I met her in the field;
She wasn't half so prim and proud,
Her own true self revealed.

Photograph © Gay Bumgarner Images/Mother-Daughter Press

At Eastertime

Ruby Lee Mitchell

Easter is still the wondrous miracle it was on that early morning centuries ago, when our Savior left empty His dark and dismal tomb.

Our hearts swell with joy when we think of the triumph of His Resurrection. It makes one realize that although one may be entombed by sin and degradation, one can emerge as white and shining as the angel who spoke those always remembered words, "He is risen. He is not here."

Eastertime is a time of rebirth. It means green things springing up, thrusting through what was snowy, frozen earth not long ago to leaf and flower.

We can sense the stirring of new life everywhere, of roots underground eager to break through their dark realms to cover the cold, brown earth with fresh new grass that gleams in the sunlight.

The bright spring flowers are pure joy. There is enchantment in watching bare drab trees as the first faint green appears; as the tiny leaves grow and grow to look like pale green smoke weaving delicate patterns against the blue spring sky; as they end at last, proudly flaunting their dark glossy full-grown leaves for the coming summer's comfort and glory. All this, too, is a miracle.

Eastertime is the sunshine and the showers and the soft blue velvet sky that for long winter months was often dull and gray.

Is there any wonder when Easter comes that we should want to change to gay and colorful array? The earth does that, and as the heart runs to meet the spring, we, too, like to meet it in dress that honors such royalty.

But most of all, above everything else, Eastertime is a refreshing of the soul, a renewal of our love for God, of our Christian fellowship, of our Christian vows.

Surely countless millions feel the same. For what other reasons would multitudes crowd the churches, cathedrals, and chapels over most of the world on Easter Sunday?

We go to receive the great blessings that Easter brings, for the belief in a risen Christ, for the special meaning that Easter has for hearts that believe.

Easter is a time for rejoicing. It is the promise and the power and the glory.

A daffodil-skirted gazebo at the White Lace Inn in Sturgeon Bay, Wisconsin. Photograph © Darryl R. Beers

The Breath of God

Myra Brooks Welch

The breath of God
Stirs to life the green and growing things
That sleep beneath the sod.
He breathes on me
And in each resurrected flower
The living Christ I see.

One Seed

Mark Weinrich

From every opened flower, the fragrance fresh,
One seed has shared its life by facing death.
Beneath the soil its withered form gave birth
And burst the earthly tomb to garden light.

From wrinkled husks transformed to verdant wings,
Springs miracle of green, a sacrifice.
And multitudes, amazed, remember Christ—
One Seed has faced our death to give us life.

Bleeding hearts blooming in the garden.
Photograph © Gay Bumgarner/Mother-Daughter Press

Upon the Springtime Dawn

Mildred Spahr Cuozzo

Full upon the springtime dawn
It comes to street and lane,
Visiting with faith and love
Those who wait again.

It wakes with us at morning
And spends the joyful day
In cheerfulness and laughter,
And yet a solemn way.

It lays its touch on cherry blooms,
Whose perfume fills the air
Like incense at the altar rail,
Where eyes are closed in prayer.

So Easter comes to every church
And walks down every aisle,
And brings the heart to gladness
With reverence and a smile.

Crab apple trees in bloom along the Trempealeau River at Independence,
Wisconsin. Photograph © Ken Dequaine Photography

Maundy Thursday
Alice Kennelly Roberts

The last meal which He ate with them,
The night before He died,
Was one which they would oft recall
When He was crucified.

He talked with them and washed
    their feet;
He gave them bread and wine,
That in remembrance they might do
The act which was divine.

"No servant greater than his Lord,"
"No love so great as this"—
The words of life preceding death
Betrayed by friendship's kiss.

So silver from Iscariot's hand
Has tinkled down the years;
Man's greed has hanged his guilty self
And drowned his deed in tears.

IN REMEMBRANCE OF ME *by Greg Olsen.*
Image © Greg Olsen

The Lord Turned and Looked Upon Peter

Elizabeth Barrett Browning

The Saviour looked on Peter. Ay, no word,
No gesture of reproach! The heavens serene,
Though heavy with armed justice, did not lean
Their thunders that way! The forsaken Lord
Looked only on the traitor. None record
What that look was, none guess: for those
 who have seen
Wronged lovers loving through a
 death-pang keen,

Or pale-cheeked martyrs smiling to a sword,
Have missed Jehovah at the judgment-call.
And Peter, from the height of blasphemy—
"I never knew this man"—did quail and fall,
As knowing straight that God, and turned free
And went out speechless from the face of all,
And filled the silence, weeping bitterly.

THE CRUCIFIXION WITH ANGELS *by Charles Le Brun.*
Photograph by Jean Schormans. Image ©
Réunion des Musées Nationaux/Art Resource, New York

Bits & Pieces

Just as spring awakens the earth and stirs it to
activity, Easter awakens the soul of man and
arouses in him a divine restlessness, a desire to
share his inner spiritual joy with others.
—*Author Unknown*

Let us live with our faces turned toward
the rising sun—the risen Son.
—*S. D. Gordon*

Faith and hope triumphant say,
Christ will rise on Easter Day.
—*Phillips Brooks*

"I am the resurrection, and the life: he that
believeth in me, though he were dead, yet
shall he live: And whosoever liveth and
believeth in me shall never die."
—*John 11:25–26*

Easter proclaims that man shall overcome all his
foes, including death itself. His pathway may lead
him through the sorrows of Gethsemane, the
pain and darkness of Calvary, nevertheless
his winter of distress will yet turn to
the spring of delight.
—Charles E. Hesselgrave

Now let the heavens be joyful,
Let earth her song begin,
Let the round world keep triumph
And all that is therein;
Let all things seen and unseen,
Their notes in gladness blend,
For Christ the Lord hath risen,
Our Joy that hath no end!
—John of Damascus

"Christ the Lord
is risen today,"
Sons of men and angels say.
Raise your joys and
triumphs high;
Sing, the heavens and earth reply.
—Charles Wesley

The Crucifixion OF Jesus

LUKE 23:33–49

And when they were come to the place, which is called Calvary, there they crucified him, and the malefactors, one on the right hand, and the other on the left.

Then said Jesus, Father, forgive them; for they know not what they do. And they parted his raiment, and cast lots. And the people stood beholding. And the rulers also with them derided him, saying, He saved others; let him save himself, if he be Christ, the chosen of God.

And the soldiers also mocked him, coming to him, and offering him vinegar, And saying, If thou be the king of the Jews, save thyself. And a superscription also was written over him in letters of Greek, and Latin, and Hebrew, THIS IS THE KING OF THE JEWS.

And one of the malefactors which were hanged railed on him, saying, If thou be Christ, save thyself and us. But the other answering rebuked him, saying, Dost not thou fear God, seeing thou art in the same condemnation? And we indeed justly; for we receive the due reward of our deeds: but this man hath done nothing amiss. And he said unto Jesus, Lord, remember me when thou comest into thy kingdom.

And Jesus said unto him, Verily I say unto thee, Today shalt thou be with me in paradise.

And it was about the sixth hour, and there was a darkness over all the earth until the ninth hour. And the sun was darkened, and the veil of the temple was rent in the midst. And when Jesus had cried with a loud voice, he said, Father, into thy hands I commend my spirit: and having said thus, he gave up the ghost.

Now when the centurion saw what was done, he glorified God, saying, Certainly this was a righteous man. And all the people that came together to that sight, beholding the things which were done, smote their breasts, and returned.

And all his acquaintance, and the women that followed him from Galilee, stood afar off, beholding these things.

Stained glass window by F. Zettler in the German Church in Stockholm, Sweden. Photograph © Anna Yu/iStockphoto

The Burial AND Resurrection

LUKE 23:50–24:12

And, behold, there was a man named Joseph, a counsellor; and he was a good man, and a just: (The same had not consented to the counsel and deed of them;) he was of Arimathaea, a city of the Jews: who also himself waited for the kingdom of God. This man went unto Pilate, and begged the body of Jesus.

And he took it down, and wrapped it in linen, and laid it in a sepulchre that was hewn in stone, wherein never man before was laid. And that day was the preparation, and the sabbath drew on. And the women also, which came with him from Galilee, followed after, and beheld the sepulchre, and how his body was laid. And they returned, and prepared spices and ointments; and rested the sabbath day according to the commandment.

Now upon the first day of the week, very early in the morning, they came unto the sepulchre, bringing the spices which they had prepared, and certain others with them. And they found the stone rolled away from the sepulchre. And they entered in, and found not the body of the Lord Jesus.

And it came to pass, as they were much perplexed thereabout, behold, two men stood by them in shining garments: And as they were afraid, and bowed down their faces to the earth, they said unto them, Why seek ye the living among the dead? He is not here, but is risen: remember how he spake unto you when he was yet in Galilee, Saying, The Son of man must be delivered into the hands of sinful men, and be crucified, and the third day rise again.

And they remembered his words, And returned from the sepulchre, and told all these things unto the eleven, and to all the rest. It was Mary Magdalene and Joanna, and Mary the mother of James, and other women that were with them, which told these things unto the apostles.

And their words seemed to them as idle tales, and they believed them not.

Then arose Peter, and ran unto the sepulchre; and stooping down, he beheld the linen clothes laid by themselves, and departed, wondering in himself at that which was come to pass.

A detail of a stained glass window in the Church of Saint Mary the Virgin in Wigton, Cumbria, England. Photograph © Stan Pritchard/Alamy

The Walk to Emmaus

Luke 24:13–32

And, behold, two of them went that same day to a village called Emmaus, which was from Jerusalem about threescore furlongs. And they talked together of all these things which had happened. And it came to pass, that, while they communed together and reasoned, Jesus himself drew near, and went with them. But their eyes were holden that they should not know him. And he said unto them, What manner of communications are these that ye have one to another, as ye walk, and are sad?

And the one of them, whose name was Cleopas, answering said unto him, Art thou only a stranger in Jerusalem, and hast not known the things which are come to pass there in these days? And he said unto them, What things? And they said unto him, Concerning Jesus of Nazareth, which was a prophet mighty in deed and word before God and all the people: And how the chief priests and our rulers delivered him to be condemned to death, and have crucified him. But we trusted that it had been he which should have redeemed Israel: and beside all this, to day is the third day since these things were done. Yea, and certain women also of our company made us astonished, which were early at the sepulchre; And when they found not his body, they came, saying, that they had also seen a vision of angels, which said that he was alive. And certain of them which were with us went to the sepulchre, and found it even so as the women had said: but him they saw not.

Then he said unto them, O fools, and slow of heart to believe all that the prophets have spoken: Ought not Christ to have suffered these things, and to enter into his glory? And beginning at Moses and all the prophets, he expounded unto them in all the scriptures the things concerning himself. And they drew nigh unto the village, whither they went: and he made as though he would have gone further. But they constrained him, saying, Abide with us: for it is toward evening, and the day is far spent. And he went in to tarry with them. And it came to pass, as he sat at meat with them, he took bread, and blessed it, and brake, and gave to them.

And their eyes were opened, and they knew him; and he vanished out of their sight.

And they said one to another, Did not our heart burn within us, while he talked with us by the way, and while he opened to us the scriptures?

The Road to Emmaus

Ida Norton Munson

Twilight. And on a dusty ribboned way
Out from Jerusalem, two travelers walked.
Gray shadows touched their feet, but deeper lay
The shadows in their hearts. They softly talked
Of days just passed, of hopeless days in view,
Of boats, of nets, the while their eyes were dim,
Of Galilee, the work they used to do;
Their voices often stilled, remembering Him.
A stranger also walked that way, and when
They sensed His nearness, some new sympathy
Assuaged their grief. Old hopes came warm again
As, in the dusk, He kept them company.
Thus, through the troubled twilight of today
Emmaus road has stretched its shining thread,
And still Christ walks beside men on the way,
To hold the light of hope, to break the bread.

Dogwood trees and daffodils along a wooded path.
Photograph © Gay Bumgarner Images/Mother-Daughter Press

The Lord Is Risen

Jessie Wilmore Murton

In the still, gray dawn, through dew-hung grass,
They sought the sepulcher, silent, lone,
Their spirits troubled with this one thought:
"Oh, who shall roll us away the stone?"

But the gray dawn fled before the light
That gleamed from a seraph's radiant face,
And blossoms sprang from his footprints when
He swung the stone from its resting place.

The grass that was lately cold and wet
Sparkled and glowed in the dawn's gold spray;
An anthem echoed from far-off heights:
"The Lord! the Lord is risen today!"

O blinded eyes! O stumbling feet!
Seeking your sepulchers, silent, lone,
Vexing your hearts—while the angel waits—
With "Who shall roll us away the stone"!

Easter

Margaret Anne Huffman

Dear God, today we celebrate
the triumph of light over dark,
day over night,
truth over lie.

We'll take this message with us
into the uncertainties of
    tomorrow,
hearing Your promise

in the songs of birds
who begin singing again
before the storm has
        fully ended.

They know all along
that clouds cover,
not banish,
the sun.

Sunrise over backwater in West Dennis, Massachusetts.
Photograph © William H. Johnson

Lost and Found

Pamela Kennedy

The story of Easter is one of redemption; the amazing grace of God reaching into His creation to seek and save the lost. John Newton, who penned the great hymn "Amazing Grace," was no stranger to this redemption.

Newton was born in London, on July 24, 1725, the only child of a British sea captain and his pious wife. When John was only seven, his mother died of consumption, and his father sent him away to boarding school. Enticed by the adventurous life of his absent father, John left school by age eleven to join him at sea. The young boy quickly adapted to life among the raucous sailors, excelling in the areas of profanity, coarseness, and debauchery.

When the elder Newton retired in 1742, John was impressed as a midshipman on *H.M.S. Harwich*, but the boy chafed under the rules and expectations of his superiors. At seventeen, rebellious and angry, he deserted. When he was eventually recaptured, he was flogged, reduced to the rate of a common seaman, and traded to the cruel captain of a slave ship headed for Africa.

After reaching port, Newton was forced into servitude and treated with brutality. Having escaped once again, he was rescued in 1748 by a sea captain acquainted with his father. On the voyage home to England, the ship encountered a violent storm. Convinced that the ship was about to capsize and sink, the twenty-three-year-old Newton called out, "Lord, have mercy upon us!" Eventually the seas subsided.

This desperate cry to the Lord was the beginning of God's work of grace in his heart. Newton married his childhood sweetheart, Mary Catlett, and began to study the Scriptures in earnest. Though he soon desired to become an evangelical preacher, it would be five years before he gave up his life as the captain of a slave ship to settle in the little town of Olney. There, in 1764, he was ordained as an Anglican priest. His popular sermons were laced with stories of his early life and the transformation God had accomplished by delivering "this old Africa blasphemer!"

In his day, congregations chanted from the Psalter, but Newton thought hymns should speak to people about the love and mercy of God. He found a like-minded soul in British poet William Cowper. Together, they published a hymnal in 1779 titled *Olney Hymns*. Among Newton's contributions was the hymn we know as "Amazing Grace." In its verses the author describes not only his former condition as "a wretch" but also the redemptive work of Christ that brought this slave trader and blasphemer through "many toils and snares" and would eventually "lead him home."

Late in his life, Newton said, "My memory is nearly gone; but I remember two things: That I am a great sinner, and that Christ is a great Savior." In his epitaph, penned just before his death in 1807, he testified that though he had once been "an infidel and libertine," he was indeed "restored" and "pardoned" by the amazing grace of Jesus Christ.

Amazing Grace

Words and lyrics by John Newton

Easter

George Herbert

Rise, heart! thy Lord is risen. Sing His praise
    Without delays
Who takes thee by the hand, that thou likewise
    With Him mayst rise—
That, as His death calcined thee to dust,
His life may make thee gold, and much more just.

Awake, my lute, and struggle for thy part
    With all thy art!
The cross taught all wood to resound His name
    Who bore the same;
His stretched sinews taught all strings what key
Is best to celebrate this most high day.

Consort both harp and lute, and twist a song
    Pleasant and long!
Or since all music is but three parts vied
    And multiplied,

Oh let thy blessed Spirit bear a part,
And make up our defects with His sweet art.

I got me flowers to strew Thy way—
I got me boughs off many a tree;
But Thou wast up by break of day,
And broughtst Thy sweets along with Thee.
The sun arising in the east,
Though he give light, and th'east perfume,
If they should offer to contest
With Thy arising, they presume.

Can there be any day but this,
Though many suns to shine endeavor?
We count three hundred, but we miss—
There is but one, and that one ever.

Sheep and spring lambs grazing in a green meadow.
Photograph © Gay Bumgarner Images/Mother-Daughter Press

Bells At Eastertime

Mamie Ozburn Odum

Ring, oh Easter bells, ring out,
Ring out the blessed story;
Ring, oh Easter bells, ring loud,
And tell the loved old story.

Ring, oh Easter bells—greet the rising sun,
For this is Easter Day.
Ring, oh Easter bells—proclaim to all
The stone is rolled away.

Ring, oh Easter bells, for His precious life;
This is a joyous time.
Ring, oh Easter bells—the Resurrection
Sweetens every chime.

Ring, oh Easter bells—let gladness reign
In hearts with every sway.
Ring, oh Easter bells, the message sweet—
This is holy Easter Day.

Easter Morning

Mona K. Guldswog

The sleeping village awakes to
    the sound of bells,
Chiming in sweetest harmony,
Floating out from tall white spires,
Glorious praise to our Lord.

Golden pathways through the misty dawn,
Breaking in lacy purity
From steepletop to cobbled lane,
The blessings of His day outpoured.

*Flowering trees flanking the First United Methodist Church
in Battle Creek, Michigan. Photograph © Darryl R. Beers*

O Sing with Joy!
Patricia Clafford

O sing with joy! Let anthems raise
In happiness and words of praise.
O sing with joy the Easter story
Of the risen Lord to glory.

O sing with joy! Retell the tale
That never can grow dim or stale,
For Easter is joy when all hearts lift
In thankfulness for His life-gift.

Easter Joy
Mary Crowell

The garden listened in the stillness
Where bloomed the lilies
    pearled with dew;
The eastern sky glowed softly bright
As fragrantly the zephyrs blew.

Suddenly the dawn was startled
By an earthquake's mighty roar,
And an angel's hands were moving
The stone before the door.

He is not here! He is risen!
Sweetest music to their ears.
The women hastened
    with the message
That had scattered all their fears.

And the glad words still are sounding,
Wafted on joy's golden wings—
Christ is risen! He is living!
Through all time the echo rings.

An apple tree blooming in spring. Photograph © Flirt/SuperStock

Easter Wish

Roy Z. Kemp

May God's blessing rest upon you
On this happy Easter Day;
May His loving arms protect you
As you go upon your way.
May His sunlight shine upon you;
May He fill your heart with song;
May you always lean upon Him,
One whose heart and arms are strong.

May you walk with surer footsteps
On the path that lies ahead;
May you see with clearer vision,
Journeying where you are led.
May you feel a little closer
To the Lord of love and peace;
May your heart sing out with gladness
And your glad song never cease.

*Tulips in Butchart Gardens in Victoria, British Columbia,
Canada. Photograph © Dale Jorgenson/SuperStock*

Easter Splendor
Verna Sparks

Bluebells in the garden,
Tulips on the lawn—
What a splendid picture
For an Easter dawn.

Jonquils golden yellow,
Hyacinth pure and white,
Lilies tall and handsome
Shining in the light.

Happiness at Easter
Sweetly tells of spring,
Thoughts of love are treasured
By every living thing.

ISBN-13: 978-0-8249-1337-3

Published by Ideals Publications, a Guideposts Company
Nashville, Tennessee
www.idealsbooks.com

Copyright © 2011 by Ideals Publications

Printed and bound in the U.S.A. Printed on Weyerhaeuser Lynx. The paper used in this publication meets the minimum requirements of American National Standard for Information Sciences—Permanence of Paper for Printed Library Materials, ANSI Z39.48-1984.

Publisher, Peggy Schaefer
Editor, Melinda L. R. Rumbaugh
Copy Editor, Debra Wright
Designer, Marisa Jackson
Permissions Editor, Patsy Jay

Cover: Photograph © Exactostock/SuperStock
Inside front cover: *The Lower Lawn, Byfleet Manor-Spring Morning, April 2004* by Charles Neal. Image © Charles Neal/SuperStock
Inside back cover: *Japanese Bridge with Irises by Fleet Manor, Surrey 1998* by Charles Neal. Image © Charles Neal/SuperStock
Art for "Bits & Pieces" by Kathy Rusynyk.
"Amazing Grace" sheet music by Dick Torrans, Melode, Inc.
In Remembrance of Me copyright © by Greg Olsen. All rights reserved. Used by permission of Greg Olsen Art Publishing, Inc., Meridian, Idaho.

ACKNOWLEDGMENTS:

BEGG, DOROTHY EVELYN. "The Last Supper." Copyright © by *Weekly Unity*. Used by permission of Unity School of Christianity. CROWELL, GRACE NOLL. "Spring Freshet" from *Songs of Hope*. Copyright © 1938 by Harper & Brothers. DICKINSON, EMILY. J74 "A lady red amid the hill" from *The Poems of Emily Dickinson*, Thomas H. Johnson, ed., Cambridge, Mass.: The Belknap Press of Harvard University Press, Copyright © 1951, 1955, 1979, 1983 by the President and Fellows of Harvard College. Reprinted by permission of the publishers and the Trustees of Amherst College. FROST, ROBERT LEE, "Spring Pools" from *The Collected Poems of Robert Frost*. Halcyon House edition, 1939, copyright © 1930 by Henry Holt & Co., copyright © 1936 by Robert Frost. HUFFMAN, MARGARET ANN. "Easter" from *Family Celebrations: Prayers, Poems and Toasts*, ed. by June Cotner. Published by Andrews McMeel Publishing, 1999. Rev. Gary W. Huffman, Heir. OAKLEY, HELEN COLWELL. "Our Treasured Traditions: Easter Preparations" from *Country Living*. Copyright © by the author, published by Vantage Press. Used by permission of Leanne M. Colwell. WELCH, MYRA BROOKS. "The Breath of God" from *The Touch of the Master's Hand* by Myra Brooks Welch. Copyright © 1943/1957 by Brethren Press, Elgin, IL. WELLS, ELIZABETH. "Kite Rite" from *US Catholic*, March 2006. Used by permission of the Claretians, Chicago, IL. OUR THANKS to the following authors or their heirs: Michelle Medlock Adams, Sam Churchill, Patricia Clafford, Lucille McBroom Crumley, Mildred Spahr Cuozzo, Marion Doyle, Mona K. Guldswog, Louise Hajek, Helen Harrington, Kay Hoffman, Reginald Holmes, Mildred Spires Jacobs, Anna Johnson, Roy Z. Kemp, Pamela Kennedy, Minnie, Klemme, Alice Leedy Mason, Ruby Lee Mitchell Boerke, Ida Norton Munson, Jessie Wilmore Murton, Mamie Ozburn Odum, Marian Paust, Alice Kennelly Roberts, J. Evelyn Smith, Verna R. Sparks, Eileen Spinelli, Nancy Byrd Turner, Mark Weinrich, Norma Wrathall, Esther York Burkholder.

Every effort has been made to establish ownership and use of each selection in this book. If contacted, the publisher will be pleased to rectify any inadvertent errors or omissions in subsequent editions.